Come on an exciting journey as we follow the Goats as they run rings around the farmer, and escape all over the farm.

A fun, repetitive tale for young children, that will give them a sense of being involved in the telling of the story as they learn what comes next.

Will the farmer ever contain them and stop them escaping and running?

Where the Goats run and they jump and they skip and they spring.

And so ends The Great Goat Run.

A lovely field with high fences and a warm comfortable shed.

Then he opens the gate and the Goats escape but he herds them down the track, and into.......

The farmer sits down and he scratches his head, these Goats won't stop escaping and something needs to be done.

So he saws and he hammers and he drills and he doesn't stop until he gets the job done.

They run and they run and they run and they run, How can we end the great goat run?

The wall isn't high enough and the Goats are now escaping.

The Goats are on the Allotment, hoovering up all the weeds, clearing them up but...

They run and they run and they run and they run and so we keep going with the great goat run.

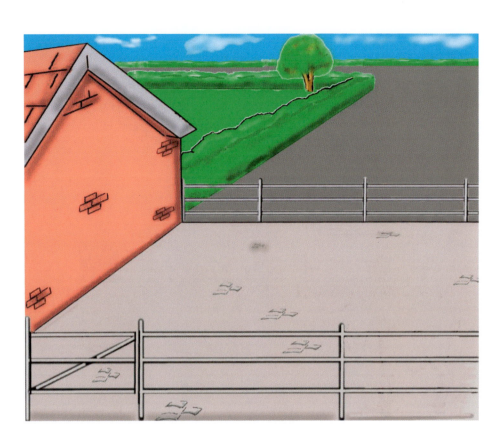

They are "Baaing" loudly and creating a fuss but then one jumps the gate, then another and another and another and they are all escaping.

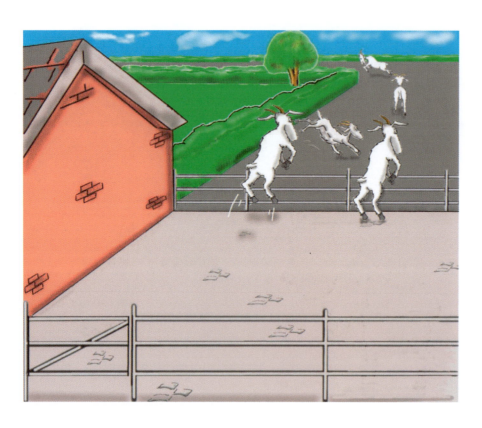

The Goats are back on the yard, waiting for the farmer, he's going to trim their feet

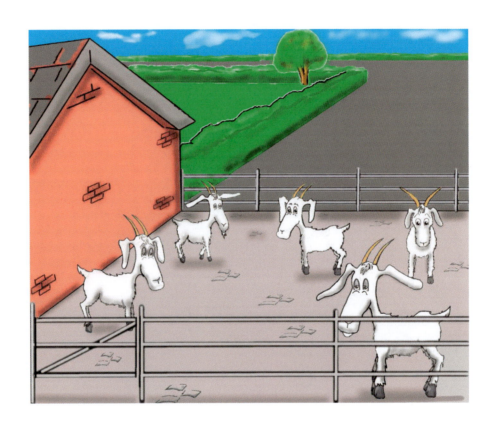

They run and they run and they run and they run and so we carry on with the great goat run.

but... They eat so much there is soon a hole in the edge and now the Goats are escaping.

The Goats are in the field nibbling on the hedges

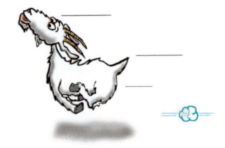

The Goats are in the milking shed all lined up for milking but...

There's a gap in the wall and the goats are now escaping.

They run and they run and they run

and they run and so continues the great goat run.

They run and they run and they run and they run and so begins the great goat run.

The Goats are in the shed, they are munching and crunching their hay but..... Someone has left the gate ajar and now the Goats are escaping.

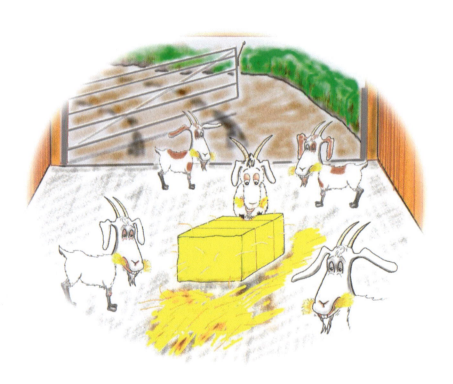

Thank you for purchasing this book, I hope it soon becomes a favourite on your bookshelf and you enjoy reading it as much as I've enjoyed writing it.

Hopefully there will be more to come and you will follow me on my dream journey, Thanks again, Alison.

This book is dedicated to Levi James and Molly May

The Great Goat Run

Written by   Alison Bailey

Illustrated by   Andrew Brough

Printed in Great Britain
by Amazon